KINGDOM Pulse

INward Awakening:

INward Death to INward Life

WORKBOOK

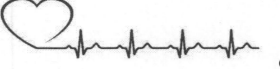

Genesis 1:1

Samantha Bishop

BK
ROYSTON
Publishing

BK Royston Publishing
P. O. Box 4321
Jeffersonville, IN 47131
502-802-5385
http://www.bkroystonpublishing.com
bkroystonpublishing@gmail.com

Cover Design: Elite Covers

ISBN-13: 978-1-951941-64-2

Printed in the United States of America

<u>Dedication</u>

This book is dedicated to the loving memory of my maternal grandfather, Pastor Samuel F. Frison. Although he is no longer with us, his legacy of Kingdom Passion remains. My passion for reading the word and writing from Father hearts was passed down to me. He served as the anchor of the Word to me as a little girl. He is forever missed but never forgotten, as I remain anchored in The Word. Papa thank you for never being perfect, but always being willing to BE perfected! You serve well in the Kingdom- and I vow to serve well with a Kingdom Pulse until it's time to BE home with Daddy God.

To Our Son:

David E. Bishop IV, our angel baby- "I will forever hold your strength as contentment dear to my heart." Thank you for being a lifeline to Mommy getting her Kingdom Pulse regulated.

To Our Daughters:

Kayla (my gift of Peace), Janiyah (my gift of Joy), and Alayna (my gift of Grace). I would not BE here today thriving with a Kingdom Pulse if you three gifts were not here with me today dwelling with The Holy Spirit. You each have such a beautiful residue of Kingdom anointing on your hearts. Always steward your Kingdom Pulse well and BE free to dance freely through life to the rhythm of Daddy God's heartbeat. May the crushing from my life lead to even greater revelation for you as you fulfill Father's Divine Purpose for your life. Love each of you more than words!!!

To the One:

The one reading this with a broken heart. I dedicate this book to you as you say Yes to Father, willing to step out of the boat that holds "what has been" to step into "what will BE"! I honor you beloved! Look no further for answers, only look to Father through this journey to your INward Awakening! Remember, giving up is NEVER an option and no matter what You can count on HIM- Our Father!

KINGDOM *Pulse*

INWARD AWAKENING:
INWARD DEATH TO INWARD LIFE

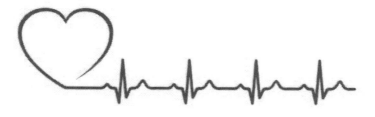

IN THE BEGINING GOD CREATED
THE HEAVENS AND THE EARTH
~GENESIS 1:1~

SAMANTHA BISHOP

The initial book, Kingdom Pulse accompanies this workbook. There will be many page number references in the workbook that will require you to have the main study book to clearly answer the questions and complete the reflections. Please visit www.sbishop2020.com to purchase the main book to move forward to be able to achieve the **IN**Ward Awakening: **IN**Ward Death to **IN**Ward Life.

Acknowledgements

First, I would like to acknowledge Daddy God for being such a faithful Father and The Holy Spirit for being the Greatest Teacher! I would not be able to fulfill my vows to Father by dying daily, without the Help of The Holy Spirit. I would also like to thank and honor my husband David for being such a great example of resilience & determination. David you have pushed me to believe **IN** and step **IN**to the impossible with Father. Thank you for reminding me of what has always been **IN** me. I love you always and forever.

It takes a village:

Therefore, I would like to honor my parents for participating with Father-birthing me into this world naturally. My Grandparents for being great examples of resilience. Next, I would like to honor my spiritual Mother (Dr. Anita Smith) for participating with Father- birthing me into the spirit realm, discipling me, & introducing me to The Holy Spirit. My mentors for always reminding me of my Kingdom Value. Honor to Kingdom counseling sent through my spiritual sister Regina, wouldn't have gotten through the last trimester of carrying Kingdom Pulse without Father's assignment on your life!

Honor to The Holy Spirit: You continue to lead hearts to the Feet of Yeshua/Jesus for divine exchanges of freedom and deliverance. Kingdom Pulse holds the residue from the healing and deliverance I personally received through a Rhema Word you anointed on April 1, 2018 from:

Isaiah 61:1 (NASB)

[1] The Spirit of the Lord GOD is upon me,

Because the LORD has anointed me

To bring good news to the afflicted;

He has sent me to bind up the brokenhearted,

To proclaim liberty to captives

And freedom to prisoners;

~ Avoidance destroys confront the spirit. Speak to the spirit-open your mouth~

I would also like to thank my editor/publisher, Julia A. Royston (BK Royston Publishing LLC) for catching the birth of Kingdom Pulse and preparing it for the Nations.

Table of Contents

Introduction

10 Points, tips and/or ways to have, get, keep and/or find the Kingdom Pulse

How do you know you have a Kingdom Pulse?

- **The Blood** — Jesus paid the cost for each of us to have a Kingdom Pulse that beats life according to Father's Divine Purpose (not according to the earthly realm). He took all your sins to the cross so that YOU could be redeemed from all bondage — INwardly and OUTwardly! Nothing you can do can change the power of The Blood that is assigned to reach you!

If your spiritual pulse was taken today, what would BE your rhythm? How can you get a regulated pulse? What steps can you take where you are?

How do you keep a Kingdom Pulse?

- **His Spirit** — We have been created in the likeness of our Father with His Spirit!

[7] For God has not given us a spirit of timidity, but of power and love and discipline.

[8] Therefore do not be ashamed of the testimony of our Lord or of me His prisoner, but join with me in suffering for the gospel according to the power of God, [9] who has saved us and called us with a holy calling, not according to our works, but according to His own purpose and grace which was granted us in Christ Jesus from all eternity, [10] but now has been revealed by the appearing of our Savior Christ Jesus, who abolished death and brought life and immortality to light through the gospel....

2 Timothy 1: 7–10, New American Standard Bible (NASB)

Nothing you can do will cancel out the orders that Father released from the beginning. He created YOU with purpose on purpose in His likeness to reveal a Kingdom Pulse that was sealed with The Blood of his only begotten son.

What is your responsibility? Partner with the Holy Spirit! How can you begin partnering with Him today?

How do you find your Kingdom Pulse?

- **Suffering** — There is a lot left in you. Father allows brokenness with intentions to help refine the diamond hidden within your heart. If you are being broken, you are being pursued.

Your life is preparing you for death (Final Destination in the Kingdom):

2 Timothy 4:7 (NASB)
I have fought the good fight, I have finished the course, I have kept the faith;

Your Kingdom Pulse will beat within until Father calls on your name to dwell with Him.
<u>Note:</u> Highly recommend investing in a *Strong's Exhaustive Concordance* as you walk out your journey to destiny. It is the tool to leverage season to season as you endure emotions sent to develop you and your relationship with Father.

Matthew 25:13 (NASB)

[13] Be on the alert then, for you do not know the day nor the hour.

In what ways are you remaining on alert (daily)? What does awareness INwardly and OUTwardly mean to you*?*

> *Daily Check:*
>
> ➢ *Journal daily what emotion and/or thought you are feeling/thinking (withholding nothing)*
> ➢ *Get your Concordance (recommend Strong's Exhaustive Concordance) and your Bible!*
> ➢ *Read your journal entry and choose ONE word that accurately describes the emotion and/or thoughts you poured out on paper.*
> ➢ *Look up that ONE word in the concordance. Pause—-Pray—Respond—Refer to each scripture listed under the word in the concordance.*
> ➢ *DO NOT just read! Take partner with the Holy Spirit with an open (consented) heart to **BE** taught! Soak your spirit man in The Word until you feel a break.*
> ➢ *Once you feel a shift and a regulation in your Kingdom Pulse, go back to the journal entry and (withholding nothing) pour out all that The Holy Spirit has poured into you regarding the emotion and/or thoughts that you are feeling*
> ➢ *Understand a shift in your unregulated Kingdom Pulse may not happen immediately, BUT it will in His timing! Remain sensitive and remain **IN** The Word postured until it does.*
> ➢ *An irregular heartbeat in the natural is not healthy and will eventually lead to complications (leading up to death). Beloved take responsibility and proper care of your spirit man! This is nobody's reasonability but yours! Don't let pride take you out painfully; submit and allow humility to take you out purposefully!*

How do you maintain a Kingdom Pulse?

- **Faith:** Your Kingdom Pulse is beating! You haven't stopped believing right!!! Through the persecutions and suffering you are postured to lie down "Who am I?" and declare "I am His"!! Doesn't mean you never wanted to give up in some seasons. It means the mustard seed of faith within was planted the moment you were paid **IN** full for by Father!! He delivered you before you needed to be delivered because His Pulse beats with**IN** you! It may be faint, but I am here to help your Kingdom Pulse get stronger so that you can live godly in Christ Jesus to BE according to His Promises!!

2 Timothy 3:10–12 (NASB)
[10] Now you followed my teaching, conduct, purpose, faith, patience, love, perseverance, [11] persecutions, and sufferings, such as happened to me at Antioch, at Iconium and at Lystra; what persecutions I endured, and out of them all the Lord rescued me! [12] Indeed, all who desire to live godly in Christ Jesus will be persecuted.

Write down the seasons you remember wanting to give up. Did you feel alone? When did you realize you had to continue believing?

Note: Invest in a Bible that speaks your language. Do you speak King James? Does Father speak King James to you? Okay then, so invest! Pray and partner with the Holy spirit so that He can guide you to the language you need to properly receive His instructions so that you follow according to understanding and not misunderstanding.

- **Hope:** If you've been rejected, this simply reveals The Kingdom Pulse withIN you! The only way to keep this pulse is understand WHO you belong to:

Luke 10:16–17 (NASB)
[16] "The one who listens to you listens to Me, and the one who rejects you rejects Me; and he who rejects Me rejects the One who sent Me." [17] The seventy returned with joy, saying, "Lord, even the demons are subject to us in Your name."

Yes, you/we as His sons and daughters (created in His likeness with His Spirit) will be rejected BUT get a revelation of this scripture. This is not a carnal perspective beloved its spiritual! The one who rejects you lacks understanding of who they are therefore they are lack understanding of The One who went to the cross to redeem us as children of Father. Your hope is found in knowing that even the demons are subject to us because of who our Father is-Yahweh!

Your Kingdom Pulse is kept because of His Blood and His Name! It may be faint at times, but it is kept by Him!!

Psalm 22:1–25 (NASB)

[1] My God, my God, why have You forsaken me?
Far from my deliverance are the words of my groaning.
[2] O my God, I cry by day, but You do not answer;
And by night, but I have no rest.
[3] Yet You are holy,
O You who are enthroned upon the praises of Israel.
[4] In You our fathers trusted;
They trusted and You delivered them.
[5] To You they cried out and were delivered;
In You they trusted and were not disappointed.
[6] But I am a worm and not a man,
A reproach of men and despised by the people.
[7] All who see me sneer at me;
They separate with the lip, they wag the head, saying,
[8] "Commit yourself to the Lord; let Him deliver him;
Let Him rescue him, because He delights in him."
[9] Yet You are He who brought me forth from the womb;
You made me trust when upon my mother's breasts.
[10] Upon You I was cast from birth;
You have been my God from my mother's womb.
[11] Be not far from me, for trouble is near;
For there is none to help.
[12] Many bulls have surrounded me;
Strong bulls of Bashan have encircled me.
[13] They open wide their mouth at me,
As a ravening and a roaring lion.
[14] I am poured out like water,
And all my bones are out of joint;
My heart is like wax;
It is melted within me.
[15] My strength is dried up like a potsherd,
And my tongue cleaves to my jaws;
And You lay me in the dust of death.
[16] For dogs have surrounded me;
A band of evildoers has encompassed me;
They pierced my hands and my feet.
[17] I can count all my bones.
They look, they stare at me;
[18] They divide my garments among them,
And for my clothing they cast lots.
[19] But You, O Lord, be not far off;

O You my help, hasten to my assistance.
[20] Deliver my soul from the sword,
My only life from the power of the dog.
[21] Save me from the lion's mouth;
From the horns of the wild oxen You answer me.

[22] I will tell of Your name to my brethren;
In the midst of the assembly I will praise You.
[23] You who fear the Lord, praise Him;
All you descendants of Jacob, glorify Him,
And stand in awe of Him, all you descendants of Israel.
[24] For He has not despised nor abhorred the affliction of the afflicted;
Nor has He hidden His face from him;
But when he cried to Him for help, He heard.
[25] From You comes my praise in the great assembly;
I shall pay my vows before those who fear Him.

Have you been impacted like David? How have you been changed (crying to rejoicing)? How have you found Joy in knowing WHO you belong to? What steps can you take to validate that you keep in mind the hope and victory that Daddy God has promised to YOU, so that you don't go back to the way YOU used to respond (at heart)?

Tips:

➤ **Keep Fighting** — No matter how difficult your situation may seem (INwardly and OUTwardly); don't give up — keep fighting, beloved!

➤ **Remain in Preparation** — get into a Holy Spirit-filled discipleship class/school/training. The only way to face death calmly INwardly and to awaken OUTwardly is through discipline!

➤ **BE Faithful** — Your response to Father is everything, beloved! Make sure your consent is from the heart to commit to learning who you are and becoming who you are through ongoing discipling. No matter what, BE found faithful to His call on your life as sons/daughters and then as a disciple of Jesus!

➤ **Protect Your Identity** — The call on your life does not define you! The destiny He has planned for you is not who you are! The anointing that MUST **BE** crushed out of your life is not who you are (prophet, apostle, teacher, shepherd, evangelist). YOU are a son or a daughter to Father! Nothing trumps that! Protect this very truth with every inch of Faith with**IN**! No matter what lane He anoints you for (season to season), your confidence according to Sonship will take the lead! You've been released from an orphan spirit; stay free!!!

➢ **<u>Invest</u>**: Investing in your spiritual health is just as important (if not more important) than investing in your physical health. Yes, we need these vessels (our temples) prepared to serve well and run the race to finish well; however, if your physical man has been given more intentional care than your spirit man, the Kingdom Race will not **BE** fulfilled. Discipleship is an ongoing process to ensure that your spirit man is thriving off meat and not milk! Once you come through discipleship remain **IN #TheWord** for yourself!! Never expect anyone to invest **IN** you! Remain under Holy Spirit-filled leaders/spiritual mothers and fathers/teachers/mentors, but never place them superior of the Greatest Helper and Protector — Father and The Holy Spirit. Invest IN time with both so that you, beloved, remain trained according to Kingdom Principle to reap Kingdom Investment.

➢ **<u>Refuse to BE Buried Alive</u>:** You have been redeemed with purpose on purpose!! Therefore, live a life daily free from needing to be validated by man. Live a life of Christ that reveals 100% partnership with Father and The Holy Spirit! Your answer and Divine Instructions come from Him alone as ONLY He knows the future. Life is a vapor beloved so don't waste it on a victim perspective or dependent perspective! You have a Kingdom Pulse, so never allow this world to bury YOU alive! YOU have work to do — **BE** found <u>At Peace</u> serving Well!

Chapter 1 — Who am I?

Make It Personal:

- **IN** what ways are you or have you wrestled with "Who am I?"

_____
_____
_____
_____
_____
_____

Ask:

- Briefly write down the emotions felt during the challenging seasons of "Who am I?"

_____
_____
_____
_____
_____
_____

- Focus **IN** on the transitioning season you were **IN**. What were some of the high and low moments — those frustrating, fearful, painful, and/or discouraging moments?

_____
_____
_____
_____
_____

- How did these those influence your identity (your "Who am I?")?

_____
_____
_____
_____
_____
_____
_____

Remember:

- Power **IN** low places — YOUR wilderness holds pain with great PURPOSE!

Discussion:

Wilderness — Greek meaning — eramos — (uncultivated places; lonely place; desert)

- What is a wilderness to you? (*List the first thought that came to mind.*)
- What did you learn from your time **IN** your wilderness (lonely place)?
- What made you feel or believe you were alone?

_____
_____
_____
_____
_____
_____
_____
_____
_____
_____
_____
_____
_____
_____
_____
_____
_____
_____
_____
_____
_____
_____
_____
_____
_____
_____
_____
_____
_____
_____
_____

Takeaway:

- Our destination is not the wilderness! We are simply passing through as we journey to Divine Purpose (Father's Destiny for us).

Ask:

What is the purpose **IN** our wilderness season?

_____

_____

_____

_____

_____

_____

_____

- **Read:**
    - ✓ Mark 1:4 & Mark 1:10–13
      (*Focus → The Heart!*)
    - ✓ Genesis 16:7–13
      (*Focus → Hagar flees to wilderness → Encounters Father → Receives Prophetic Word.*)
    - ✓ Exodus 4:27
      (*Focus →Aaron meets Moses IN the wilderness →Divine Encounter → Divine Exchange → Divine Purpose*)
    - ✓ 1 Samuel 23:14
      (*Focus → David Stayed IN the wilderness → Pursued by enemy → Divine Protection*)
    - ✓ 1 Samuel 25:4
      (*Focus → David listened IN the wilderness →Wisdom Received → Warning Received*)

- **Reading Takeaways**:

    - ✓ Power & Purpose **IN** low places.
    - ✓ Our **INNER** most needs are identified and met IN our time in "lonely places."
    - ✓ Repentance → Reverence → Relationship established IN our Wilderness
      (*pg 89 Kingdom Pulse will provide deeper understanding*)
    - ✓ Our "condition" **IN**wardly takes us to low places.
    - ✓ The feet of Father is where we cry out and receive!

_____

_____

_____

_____

Reflection:

1. What do you hear The Holy Spirit speaking to you where you are?

_____
_____
_____
_____
_____
_____
_____
_____
_____

2. Are you aware of the pain **IN**wardly? Has this led to you feeling buried alive (state of hopelessness)?

_____
_____
_____
_____
_____
_____
_____
_____
_____

3. What Divine Exchange are you expecting through your journey through Kingdom Pulse?

_____
_____
_____
_____
_____
_____
_____
_____
_____
_____
_____
_____

INward Challenge:

Before transitioning to Chapter 2 declaring "I am His."

1.   Write out transparently the raw thoughts and pain that you had or have before you were led to be assessed through Kingdom Pulse.

_____

_____

_____

_____

_____

_____

2.   Write out every emotion (anger frustration, guilt, uncertainty, fear, doubt, shame, jealousy, envy, hate, etc.).

_____

_____

_____

_____

_____

_____

_____

3.   When you ask yourself "Who am I?" what immediate response arises?

_____

_____

_____

_____

_____

_____

4.   Get a Concordance and look up the emotions you listed.

_____

_____

_____

_____

_____

_____

_____

_____

_____

5.   Refer to scripture aligned to each emotion. Align how you feel (what you wrote) to what The Word says!

_____
_____
_____
_____
_____
_____
_____
_____
_____

6.   Now journal what Father says about every emotion you are facing **IN** the "lonely place."

_____
_____
_____
_____
_____
_____
_____
_____
_____
_____
_____
_____
_____
_____
_____
_____
_____
_____
_____
_____

Psalm 56:9 Amplified Bible (AMP)

[9] Then my enemies will turn back in the day when I call;

This I know, that God is for me.

__Reflection__

_____
_____
_____
_____
_____
_____
_____
_____
_____
_____
_____
_____
_____
_____
_____
_____
_____
_____
_____
_____
_____
_____
_____
_____
_____
_____
_____
_____

<u>Reflection</u>

_____
_____
_____
_____
_____
_____
_____
_____
_____
_____
_____
_____
_____
_____
_____
_____
_____
_____
_____
_____
_____
_____
_____
_____
_____
_____
_____
_____
_____
_____
_____

Chapter 2 — INward Awakening

Make It Personal:

- What did or do I have **IN** mind?

_____
_____
_____
_____
_____
_____
_____

- Is my heart IN a condition to Fight (through my response **IN**wardly)?

_____
_____
_____
_____
_____
_____
_____

- What is Father's desire for me as His son/daughter? (*See pg. 56.*)

_____
_____
_____
_____
_____
_____

- Am I facing uncertainty about my relationship with God? Do I believe? (*See pg. 64–66.*)

_____
_____
_____
_____
_____
_____
_____

Ask:

- Why is your willingness to give up what you have **IN** mind critical to **IN**ward Awakening? (*See pg. 32.*)

_____
_____
_____
_____
_____
_____
_____

- Are you ready to go from vowing to understanding how to **IN**wardly pay?

_____
_____
_____
_____
_____
_____
_____
_____

Get Understanding:

- What is the first step to awakening as "I am His"? (*See pg. 35.*)

_____
_____
_____
_____
_____
_____
_____

- What is the purpose of Chapter 2? (*See pg. 36.*)

_____
_____
_____
_____
_____
_____

- What is the first step to **IN**ward Awakening?

_____
_____
_____
_____
_____

INward Challenge:

1.   What is Flight or Fight Response? (*See pg. 36.*)

_____

_____

_____

_____

_____

_____

_____

2.   Why is it important to understand my trained response? (*See pg. 37.*)

_____

_____

_____

_____

_____

_____

_____

3.   Do I have or have I had a Flight Response? (*See pg. 39.*)

_____

_____

_____

_____

_____

_____

_____

4.   What does Flight response look like **IN** me? (*See pg. 40–46.*)

_____

_____

_____

_____

_____

_____

_____

_____

_____

_____

_____

5.   According to scripture what should a Fight response **BE IN** and revealed through me? (*See pg. 40–46*)

_____
_____
_____
_____
_____
_____
_____
_____
_____

Takeaways:

➢ When our speech is motivated by Satan, it is full of what? (*See pg. 49–50.*)

_____
_____
_____
_____
_____
_____
_____
_____

➢ When our speech is motivated by God, it is full of what? (*See pg. 50.*)

_____
_____
_____
_____
_____
_____
_____
_____

➢ What are the types of Spiritual Heart Conditions? (*See pg. 51–52.*)

_____
_____
_____
_____
_____
_____
_____
_____
_____
_____

➢ What are three required essentials to spiritually Fight effectively? (*See pg. 52–53.*)

_____

_____

_____

_____

_____

Take Responsibility:

1. What has triggered my heart condition spiritually? (*See pg. 54.*)

_____

_____

_____

_____

_____

2. How is my heart condition diagnosed spiritually? What steps can I **BE**gin to take to open areas of my heart that reveal blockage? (*See pg. 55–56.*)

_____

_____

_____

_____

_____

_____

3. How can my heart condition **BE** stabilized spiritually?

_____

_____

_____

_____

_____

4. What happens if my heart is not stabilized spiritually? (*See pg. 58–59.*)

_____

_____

_____

_____

_____

5. What does your spiritual assessment reveal today? (*See pg. 60.*)

_____
_____
_____
_____
_____
_____
_____

6. What am I trusting **IN**?

_____
_____
_____
_____
_____
_____
_____
_____

~ Remember, Beloved ~

John 1:1-3 (AMP)

[1] In the beginning (before all time) was the Word (Christ), and the Word was with God, and the Word was God Himself. [2] He was (continually existing) in the beginning (co-eternally) with God. [3] All things were made and came into existence through Him; and without Him not even one thing was made that has come into being.

Role of the Spirit

John 14:15—6 (AMP)

[15] If you (really) love Me, you will keep and obey My commandments.

[16] And I will ask the Father, and He will give you another Helper (Comforter, Advocate, Intercessor—Counselor, Strengthener, Standby), to be with you forever—

Romans 8:13–14 (AMP)

[13] for if you are living according to the (impulses of the) flesh, you are going to die. But if (you are living) by the (power of the Holy) Spirit you are habitually putting to death the sinful deeds of the body, you will [really] live forever. [14] For all who are allowing themselves to be led by the Spirit of God are sons of God.

1 Corinthians 6:17 (NASB)

[17] But the one who joins himself to the Lord is one spirit with Him.

Galatians 5:16 (AMP)

[16] But I say, walk habitually in the (Holy) Spirit (seek Him and be responsive to His guidance), and then you will certainly not carry out the desire of the sinful nature (which responds impulsively without regard for God and His precepts).

Fill in the Blank:

Fear will execute a _____ **RESPONSE.**

Faith will execute a _____ **RESPONSE.**

Both reveal a "type" of trust → only one can deliver/awaken our INNER man.

Psalm 20:7 (AMP)

[7] Some trust in chariots and some in horses, But we will remember and trust in the name of the Lord our God.

<u>Reflection</u>

_____
_____
_____
_____
_____
_____
_____
_____
_____
_____
_____
_____
_____
_____
_____
_____
_____
_____
_____
_____
_____
_____
_____
_____
_____
_____
_____
_____

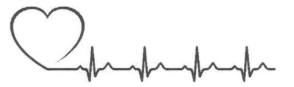

<u>Reflection</u>

_____
_____
_____
_____
_____
_____
_____
_____
_____
_____
_____
_____
_____
_____
_____
_____
_____
_____
_____
_____
_____
_____
_____
_____
_____
_____
_____
_____
_____

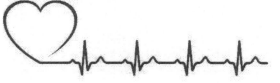

Reflection

_____
_____
_____
_____
_____
_____
_____
_____
_____
_____
_____
_____
_____
_____
_____
_____
_____
_____
_____
_____
_____
_____
_____
_____
_____
_____
_____
_____
_____
_____
_____
_____

Chapter 3 — Alignment

Make It Personal:

- How do I activate my ticket to onboard a Flight to His destiny for me? (*See pg. 69.*)

_____
_____
_____
_____
_____
_____
_____

- Am I Being a representative of His Church (as a son/daughter 1st)?

_____
_____
_____
_____
_____
_____
_____

- Which church (heart response) am I aligned to NOW?

_____
_____
_____
_____
_____
_____
_____

- Am I truly living as **BE**ing **IN** alignment with the heart of God (as your Father)?

_____
_____
_____
_____
_____
_____
_____
_____

Ask:

1. List five Key Points to remaining **IN** alignment to Destiny. (*See pg. 80–85.*)

_____
_____
_____
_____
_____
_____
_____
_____
_____

2. List the "3 R's" (*See pg. 89.*)

_____
_____
_____
_____
_____
_____
_____
_____
_____

3. **IN** what ways are you **IN** alignment to the "3 R's"? **IN** what ways are you out of alignment?

_____
_____
_____
_____
_____
_____
_____
_____
_____

Get Understanding:

➢ What is submission? (*See pg. 90.*)

_____
_____
_____
_____
_____
_____
_____
_____
_____

➤ When did Father begin His mission (assignment) in the Bible? (*See pg. 90.*)

_____

_____

_____

_____

_____

_____

_____

➤ Why is it important to under The Assignment of The Holy Spirit (abide to)? (*See pg. 91.*)

_____

_____

_____

_____

_____

_____

_____

➤ The continued process of submission consists of: (*See pg. 92–94.*) → List three processes.

_____

_____

_____

_____

_____

_____

_____

➤ What are the seven churches that will **BE** judged by Father? (*See pg. 83.*)

_____

_____

_____

_____

_____

_____

_____

Psalm 139:23–24 (AMP)

[23] Search me (thoroughly), O God, and know my heart;

Test me and know my anxious thoughts;

[24] And see if there is any wicked or hurtful way in me,

And lead me in the everlasting way.

<u>Reflection</u>

_____
_____
_____
_____
_____
_____
_____
_____
_____
_____
_____
_____
_____
_____
_____
_____
_____
_____
_____
_____
_____
_____
_____
_____
_____
_____
_____
_____
_____
_____
_____
_____

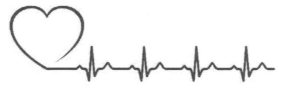

<u>Reflection</u>

_____

_____

_____

_____

_____

_____

_____

_____

_____

_____

_____

_____

_____

_____

_____

_____

_____

_____

_____

_____

_____

_____

_____

_____

_____

_____

_____

_____

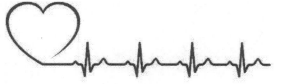

__Reflection__

_____
_____
_____
_____
_____
_____
_____
_____
_____
_____
_____
_____
_____
_____
_____
_____
_____
_____
_____
_____
_____
_____
_____
_____
_____
_____
_____
_____
_____
_____
_____
_____
_____

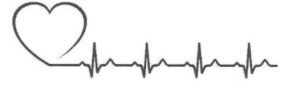

Chapter 4 — Taking Responsibility #TheHeart

Make It Personal:

- How is/has the condition of my heart influenced my ability to endure seasons (by Faith)?

_____
_____
_____
_____
_____
_____

- Am I equipped to strive with His immediate Response (led by The Holy Spirit)?

_____
_____
_____
_____
_____
_____

- Is my heart in the condition to get up and **BE**gin to walk out Destiny?

_____
_____
_____
_____
_____

- Am I spiritually equipped to respond to **IN**ward adversity that comes with ordained victory?

_____
_____
_____
_____
_____
_____
_____
_____
_____
_____

Ask:

1. Why is Father intentionally stepping into our hearts? What is He reminding us of? *(See pg. 98.)*

_____

_____

_____

_____

_____

_____

2. Avoidance is a response rooted **IN** _____ and/or _____. *(See pg. 99.)*

_____

_____

_____

_____

_____

_____

3. What are you fearing or avoiding **IN**wardly?

_____

_____

_____

_____

_____

_____

4. What does James 5:17 tell us? How is your prayer life? *(See pg. 99.)*

_____

_____

_____

_____

_____

_____

5. Who was Elijah? Who was Ahab? Who Was Jezebel?

_____

_____

_____

_____

_____

_____

_____

6. Why was Jezebel angry? What was the purpose of her pursuit for Elijah?

_____

_____

_____

_____

_____

7. What was Elijah's **heart** response to victory? Did he have a Flight Response or Fight Response? *(See pg. 101.)*

_____

_____

_____

_____

_____

_____

8. What two types of posture can an avoidance spirit lead to? *(See pg. 103.)*

_____

_____

_____

_____

_____

_____

9. What type of posture do you have **IN** this season?

_____

_____

_____

_____

_____

_____

Understand:

✓ What state/condition did Elijah have to **BE** pulled out of? *(See pg. 104.)*

_____

_____

_____

_____

_____

_____

✓ 1 Kings 19:3 reveals that Father let Elijah do what? (*See pg. 104.*)

_____

_____

_____

_____

_____

_____

✓ Did Father excuse Elijah from the Divine Instructions assigned to his destiny? (*See pg. 104.*)

_____

_____

_____

_____

_____

_____

_____

Psalm 27:4 (AMP)

[4] One thing I have asked of the Lord, and that I will seek:

That I may dwell in the house of the Lord (in His presence) all the days of my life,

To gaze upon the beauty (the delightful loveliness and majestic grandeur]) of the Lord

And to meditate in His temple.

Reflection

_____
_____
_____
_____
_____
_____
_____
_____
_____
_____
_____
_____
_____
_____
_____
_____
_____
_____
_____
_____
_____
_____
_____
_____
_____
_____
_____
_____

<u>Reflection</u>

_____
_____
_____
_____
_____
_____
_____
_____
_____
_____
_____
_____
_____
_____
_____
_____
_____
_____
_____
_____
_____
_____
_____
_____
_____
_____
_____
_____
_____
_____
_____
_____

Chapter 5 — Be at Peace

Make It Personal:

- Why am I postured here today? (*See pg.119.*)

_____

_____

_____

_____

_____

_____

- Am I **IN** a current posture of doubt, anger, complacency, etc.

_____

_____

_____

_____

_____

_____

- Am I willing to give up what I have **IN** mind?

_____

_____

_____

_____

_____

_____

- What attitude have I been serving with? (*See pg.126.*)

_____

_____

_____

_____

_____

_____

- Am I aware of ow to get to the place Jesus has prepared for me? (*See pg.130.*)

_____

_____

_____

_____

Ask:

➤ What comes to mind when you hear or see the "phrase"→ **Be at Peace**? (*See pg.121*)

_____
_____
_____
_____
_____
_____

➤ What does it mean to **#BE?** (*See pg.121.*)

_____
_____
_____
_____
_____
_____

➤ Why did Paul warn to guard #**TheHear**t? (*See pg.126–127.*)

_____
_____
_____
_____
_____
_____

➤ Is **AT** a location? If so, where can we refer to this location? (*See pg.129.*)

_____
_____
_____
_____
_____
_____

➤ Why is the Sacred Place within vital to our daily walk (sons/daughters)? (*See pg.133.*)

_____
_____
_____
_____
_____
_____
_____

➤ Why is deliverance and discipleship required to remain **#AT** the sacred place within? (*See pg.134–135.*)

_____

_____

_____

_____

_____

_____

_____

_____

Activity:

Refer to The Sermon on The Mount; The Beatitudes. (*See pg.127.*)

✓ <u>Step 1</u> — List each verse by number
✓ <u>Step 2</u> — Following "Blessed are" ask yourself if your attitude has been aligned to reveal a posture of those who are "poor in spirit," "who mourn," "are gentle," "who hunger and thirst for righteousness," etc.
✓ <u>Step 3</u> — In a brief summary, discuss how your beatitude is/has been **IN** or out of alignment to His Word? (*See pg.126*)
✓ <u>Step 4</u> — What steps do you plan to take to influence your obtaining a heart transplant and renewed mind?

_____

_____

_____

_____

_____

_____

_____

_____

_____

_____

_____

_____

Psalm 34:17-18 (NASB)

17 The righteous cry, and the Lord hears

And delivers them out of all their troubles.

18 The Lord is near to the brokenhearted

And saves those who are crushed in spirit.

Reflection

_____
_____
_____
_____
_____
_____
_____
_____
_____
_____
_____
_____
_____
_____
_____
_____
_____
_____
_____
_____
_____
_____
_____
_____
_____
_____
_____
_____
_____
_____

<u>Reflection</u>

_____
_____
_____
_____
_____
_____
_____
_____
_____
_____
_____
_____
_____
_____
_____
_____
_____
_____
_____
_____
_____
_____
_____
_____
_____
_____

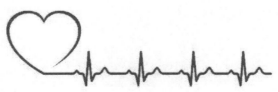

<u>**Reflection**</u>

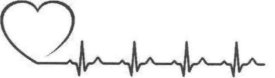

Chapter 6 — Listen to Follow

Pre-Work:

- What is the role of The Holy Spirit?

_____

_____

_____

_____

_____

_____

- What bird represents The Holy Spirit?

_____

_____

_____

_____

_____

_____

Fill in The Blank:

- Jesus was led by _____ into the _____ to be _____ by the _____. (*See pg. 140.*)
- Following Father's_____ should remain the _____focus and _____. (*See pg. 145.*)
- **LISTEN TO** _____ to remain bold in the midst of persecution! (*See pg. 146.*)
- **LISTEN TO** _____ to remain postured at heart (_____)!
- Blessed is the one who _____ to _____ to _____ of Daddy God. (*See pg.146.*)

Make It Personal:

✓ Who are you Being led by?

_____

_____

_____

_____

_____

✓ Where have you been led to (at this point/season)?

_____
_____
_____
_____
_____
_____
_____

✓ What has the enemy used or is using to lead you into temptation IN your life?

_____
_____
_____
_____
_____
_____
_____
_____

Understand:

➢ Temptation has no power! What does temptation have (*fill in the blank*) _____. (*See pg. 141.*)

Ask:

1. Why did Father not only give us all power and authority but access to His Helper (The Holy Spirit)?

_____
_____
_____
_____
_____
_____
_____

2. According to scripture, "For it is not you who speak, but it is the Spirit of your Father who speaks in you. (Matt. 10:20, NASB)."

_____
_____
_____
_____
_____
_____
_____
_____
_____

3. Are you listening to follow, beloved? How can you BE more sensitive to His Spirit? (*See pg. 144.*)

_____

_____

_____

_____

_____

_____

_____

_____

Matthew 6:33 (NASB)

[33] But [a]seek first [b]His kingdom and His righteousness, and all these things will be [c]added to you.

<u>Reflection</u>

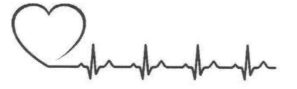

Reflection

_____
_____
_____
_____
_____
_____
_____
_____
_____
_____
_____
_____
_____
_____
_____
_____
_____
_____
_____
_____
_____
_____
_____
_____
_____
_____
_____

<u>Reflection</u>

_____
_____
_____
_____
_____
_____
_____
_____
_____
_____
_____
_____
_____
_____
_____
_____
_____
_____
_____
_____
_____
_____
_____
_____
_____
_____
_____
_____
_____
_____

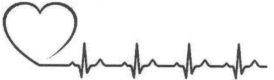

Chapter 7 — Remain (Whole)!

Make It Personal:

- Describe how you have invested IN His Plan and Purpose of Rest IN you.

_____
_____
_____
_____
_____
_____
_____

Ask:

- What does it mean to rest?

_____
_____
_____
_____
_____
_____

- List four expressions of rest. (*See pg. 150–155.*)
    1. _____
    2. _____
    3. _____
    4. _____

- What five key focus points reveal our responsibility of rest? (*See pg. 156–159.*)

    Note: First Letter of Answer Provided

    1. C_____
    2. T_____
    3. T_____
    4. R_____
    5. U_____

- Who is our only source of Rest? (*See pg. 160–162.*)

    *Answer:*_____ & _____

- What distracts us from Resting **IN**wardly? (*See pg. 163–164.*)

    1. S_____
    2. R_____
    3. P_____
    4. A_____

- List four key steps to renewing strength Inwardly. (*See pg.164–165.*)

    1. _____
    2. _____
    3. _____
    4. _____

Colossians 3:2-3 (NASB)

[2] Set your mind on the things above,

not on the things that are on earth. [3]

For you have died and your life is hidden

with Christ in God.

<u>Reflection</u>

_____
_____
_____
_____
_____
_____
_____
_____
_____
_____
_____
_____
_____
_____
_____
_____
_____
_____
_____
_____
_____
_____
_____
_____
_____
_____
_____
_____
_____

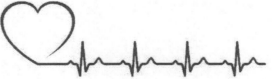

Reflection

_____
_____
_____
_____
_____
_____
_____
_____
_____
_____
_____
_____
_____
_____
_____
_____
_____
_____
_____
_____
_____
_____
_____
_____
_____
_____
_____
_____
_____
_____

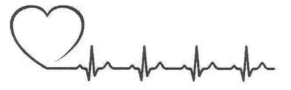

Chapter 8 — Process of Partnership

Make It Personal:

- In your own words — Describe what the Process of Partnership looks like from a current perspective? (*See pg. 170 for takeaways.*)

_____

_____

_____

_____

_____

_____

- Have you submitted your life into the Potter's hand? List what ways you surrender (daily) to grow **IN** His Grace.

_____

_____

_____

_____

_____

_____

_____

- What ways can you begin a process of surrendering daily to grow **IN** His Grace?

_____

_____

_____

_____

_____

_____

- Are YOU #AT peace with accepting the good as well as the adversity that comes with Being a son/daughter of Daddy God?

_____

_____

_____

_____

_____

_____

_____

_____

- What are YOU willing to give up to live out The Promises of Daddy God?

_____

_____

_____

_____

_____

_____

_____

_____

_____

Fill in The Blank:

1. This is a process that comes with _____, _____, and _____ **IN** Father. (*See pg. 170.*)

2. Our partnership with Father is built on our ability to have Peaceful Submission to: (*See pg. 170–184.*)

   ➤ _____
   ➤ _____
   ➤ _____
   ➤ _____
   ➤ _____
   ➤ _____
   ➤ _____

3. Giving up the right to do something (surrendering) leads to blessings of: (*See pg. 185–188*)

   ➤ _____
   ➤ _____
   ➤ _____
   ➤ _____

4. Entrance into The Kingdom of God by: (*See pg. 188–190.*)

   ➤ _____
   ➤ _____
   ➤ _____
   ➤ _____

5. As Members of The Kingdom we: (*See pg. 190.*)

➢ _____

➢ _____

➢ _____

➢ _____

➢ _____

Colosssians 3:12-17 (NASB)

[12] So, as those who have been chosen of God, holy and beloved,

put on a heart of compassion, kindness, humility, gentleness and [a]patience;

[13] bearing with one another, and forgiving each other, whoever has a complaint against anyone;

just as the Lord forgave you, so also should you.

[14] Beyond all these things *put on* love, which is [b]the perfect bond of unity.

[15] Let the peace of Christ [c]rule in your hearts, to which [d]indeed you were called

in one body; and [e]be thankful. [16] Let the word of [f]Christ richly dwell within you,

[g]with all wisdom teaching and admonishing [h]one another with
psalms *and* hymns *and* spiritual

songs, singing [i]with thankfulness in your hearts to God. [17] Whatever you do in word or

deed, *do* all in the name of the Lord Jesus, giving thanks through Him to God the Father.

Reflection

_____
_____
_____
_____
_____
_____
_____
_____
_____
_____
_____
_____
_____
_____
_____
_____
_____
_____
_____
_____
_____
_____
_____
_____
_____
_____
_____
_____
_____
_____
_____

<u>Reflection</u>

_____
_____
_____
_____
_____
_____
_____
_____
_____
_____
_____
_____
_____
_____
_____
_____
_____
_____
_____
_____
_____
_____
_____
_____
_____
_____
_____
_____

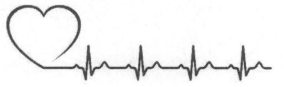

<u>Reflection</u>

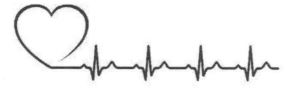

Chapter 9 — Be Available

Make It Personal:

- In what ways do areas of your life reveal lack of faith & obedience?

_____
_____
_____
_____
_____
_____

- Are you available (**IN**wardly) — aligned to (prepared for) Father's promises?

_____
_____
_____
_____
_____
_____

Ask:

1. What does it mean to be an heir of God? (*See pg. 194.*)

_____
_____
_____
_____
_____

2. What does "Sold" mean? (*See pg. 195.*)

_____
_____
_____
_____
_____
_____
_____
_____

Fill in the Blank:

➤ We share **IN** the _____ of _____ now and will _____ **IN** the Glory of _____ later. (*See pg. 194.*)

➤ Self-Denial can be revealed through: (*See pg. 208–210.*)

_____

_____

_____

_____

_____

_____

➤ Self-Denial is honored as: (*See pg. 211–212.*)

_____

_____

Activity:

Scripture Focus (*See pg.195.*)

- <u>Step 1</u> — Using your Bible, reference each scripture (one at a time).
- <u>Step 2</u> — Pause after reading each verse.
- <u>Step 3</u> — Journal what each verse is speaking to YOU **IN** this season.
- <u>Step 4</u> — List how you haven't made room **IN** your heart for Father.
- <u>Step 5</u> — List how you plan to prepare room **IN** your heart for Father.

_____

_____

_____

_____

_____

_____

_____

_____

_____

_____

_____

_____

Reflection

_____
_____
_____
_____
_____
_____
_____
_____
_____
_____
_____
_____
_____
_____
_____
_____
_____
_____
_____
_____
_____
_____
_____
_____
_____
_____

Reflection

Chapter 10 — All Things Are Passed Away

Make It Personal

- You have a Kingdom Pulse — What does this mean to YOU?

_____

_____

_____

_____

_____

_____

- You Are His Revival — What does this mean to YOU?

_____

_____

_____

_____

_____

_____

Ask:

1. The only response that matters is the response that comes from Whom? (*See pg. 216.*)

_____

_____

_____

_____

_____

2. True or False (circle): Absolutely nothing can cancel His Love for YOU, as a son/daughter that YOU are to Him. (*See pg. 217.*)

_____

_____

_____

_____

_____

_____

Final Activity:

- <u>Step 1</u> — Now that you have completed you journey through Kingdom Pulse — take time to reflect.
- <u>Step 2</u> — Journal where you were postured before reading vs. after reading. (Make This Personal!)
- <u>Step 3</u> — What areas **IN**wardly need or needed revived?
- <u>Step 4</u> — Invest time and obedience — Get enrolled into a Kingdom Rooted discipleship ministry.

(Recommended Discipleship Ministry: *The Christ Learning Center Ministries*)

Hebrews 12:7-17 (NASB)

[7] It is for discipline that you endure; God deals with you as with sons; for what son is there whom *his* father does not discipline? [8] But if you are without discipline, of which all have become partakers, then you are illegitimate children and not sons. [9] Furthermore, we had earthly fathers to discipline us, and we respected them; shall we not much rather be subject to the Father of spirits, and live? [10] For they disciplined us for a short time as seemed best to them, but He *disciplines us* for *our* good, so that we may share His holiness. [11] All discipline for the moment seems not to be joyful, but sorrowful; yet to those who have been trained by it, afterwards it yields the peaceful fruit of righteousness.
[12] Therefore, strengthen the hands that are weak and the knees that are feeble, [13] and make straight paths for your feet, so that *the limb* which is lame may not be put out of joint, but rather be healed. [14] Pursue peace with all men, and the sanctification without which no one will see the Lord. [15] See to it that no one comes short of the grace of God; that no root of bitterness springing up causes trouble, and by it many be defiled; [16] that *there be* no immoral or godless person like Esau, who sold his own birthright for a *single* meal. [17] For you know that even afterwards, when he desired to inherit the blessing, he was rejected, for he found no place for repentance, though he sought for it with tears.

Reflection

_____
_____
_____
_____
_____
_____
_____
_____
_____
_____
_____
_____
_____
_____
_____
_____
_____
_____
_____
_____
_____
_____
_____
_____
_____
_____
_____
_____
_____

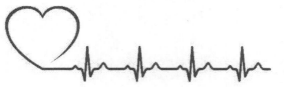

Reflection

_____
_____
_____
_____
_____
_____
_____
_____
_____
_____
_____
_____
_____
_____
_____
_____
_____
_____
_____
_____
_____
_____
_____
_____
_____
_____
_____
_____
_____
_____

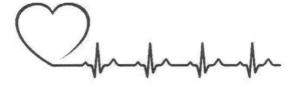

About the Author

Samantha J. Bishop

Daughter • Disciple • Reformer

e: kingdompulse@sbishop2020.com |

w: http://www.sbishop2020.com |

Samantha Bishop LLC

3100 East 45th Street, Suite 234 #525

Cleveland, Ohio 44127

Samantha J. Bishop is a creative innovator, teacher-communicator, a devoted wife, mother, author, and minister of the Gospel. She has spent the last decade investing in women, men, and young people of all ages. Her mission and focus have been on calling people into "INward" transformation and reformation by yielding to the Father's hands.

Samantha is a woman who is not only called to the ministry but is also called to minister to God's children in the marketplace and in all spheres of life.

For the last 17 years, Samantha has spent her time serving in the marketplace, as a Medical Assistant, a Recruiter, a Supervisor, a Director and currently as an Executive in Human Resources with Target. She is a woman who has seen many testimonies of healings, encounters with the Father's heart, and transformed coworkers and customers alike.

With a background in leading discipleship courses for those in all stages of their spiritual walk, Samantha can speak to both the new believer and the seasoned follower in a way that calls both higher. Each person she ministers to cannot leave without knowing that they have encountered the Father's love and the Shepherd 's gentle correction.

She pairs a broad range of creative leadership experience in leadership training & development, operation management, and recruiting with a deep understanding of psychological principle to empower great leadership that can be leveraged to drive excellence that is guaranteed to thrive personal and professional brands.

Samantha studied psychology at University of Phoenix. She is currently pursuing her Bachelor of Science in Biblical Studies at Indiana Wesleyan University.

Currently based in Cincinnati, OH, Samantha seeks to share her expertise and utilize her teacher-communicator anointing to drive leadership development, ministry collaboration, and operational strategies among the Body of Christ.

Made in the USA
Monee, IL
29 March 2021